The Brand New Dark

MARK WALDRON was born in New York and grew up in London. He writes adverts for a living and lives in east London with his wife and son. *The Brand New Dark* is his first collection.

The Brand New Dark

MARK WALDRON

SALT

CAMBRIDGE

PUBLISHED BY SALT PUBLISHING
14a High Street, Fulbourn, Cambridge, CB21 5DH United Kingdom

© Mark Waldron, 2008

The right of Mark Waldron to be identified as the
author of this work has been asserted by him in accordance
with Section 77 of the Copyright, Designs and Patents Act 1988.

First published 2008

Printed and bound in the United Kingdom by MPG Biddles Ltd, King's Lynn, Norfolk

Typeset in Swift 9.5 / 13

ISBN 978 1 84471 344 8 hardback

Salt Publishing Ltd gratefully acknowledges
the financial assistance of Arts Council England

1 3 5 7 9 8 6 4 2

For Julie

Contents

Acknowledgements

Some of these poems, or versions of them, have appeared in *Magma*, *The North*, *Poetry London*, *The Rialto*, *Rising* and *Smiths Knoll*.

I'd like to thank John Stammers and Esther Morgan for their advice on many of these poems, my wife Julie and friend David Godfree for their always invaluable opinions and above all Roddy Lumsden for his help in putting this book together. I'd also like to acknowledge the support and encouragement of the late Michael Donaghy.

Underneath the Gone Sky

they stood, stretched with relief and fear,
the spilt night over everything.

The wall she was against was on the world's edge,
her back against her shirt, her shirt against her coat,

her coat against the brick, its knuckle grit holding her on.
And beneath unspeaking clothes, he found her

hopelessly bare, peaceful, shocked,
as though her clothes had been her skin,

her skin, flesh. I promise
they were absolutely ruined by its magic.

For Them There's Nothing

They can never ride from Karlova Ves to Spitalska,
watching other trams and pale stones of faces

sunk under the glass; they can't have an itchy insect bite,
an awful cold, or let their sleepy, humid gaze

rest upon their feet beneath the water in the bath.
The things we make, the TV shows that leave

these muted traces of their colours on our clothes,
the foreign films that float below

the stripped out letters of their subtitles,
the songs we listen to and sing, none of these are for them.

They don't go out to eat, not even in the sullen,
almost empty cafés, where the world's bright juice

runs in hell-bent rivers between and through the tables
and shines on the floor and goes out onto

the green-grey street where it will rain later
and the false ceiling of cloud is lit from above;

they can't go out into the garden and turn to look up
at the curtained windows of the bedroom;

they never smell the plain wood of the boxes
we install them in and never even see the only true dark.

Dog

I had thought of you as I lay fighting
off this sleep. Now I find you as you squat
my dream as a dog. A dark bitch biting
on my dream's air. Its fur, like your hair cropped,
its teeth as white as yours, its mouth as wet.
And soon, when I awake to the new day,
you will be gone, but I will not forget
the sweet scent of you which I know will stray
between this sleeping and their wakeful place.
And now you come and look in my dog eye
and know that you don't want a man's embrace
and know that you don't want this love to die.
So sleep my bitch, within this sleep of ours
and dream within our dream through our dog hours.

At the Official Function, Captain Green,

hard as nails, wonderful hard,
utters: Mrs Spat, let me speak these brown and blue,

these wet and liberated stones, let me drip them from my lips,
to clatter sweetly in your ear, to rumble through your memory

and then to topple to your tongue, these amaranthine candies,
which then will taste of your unfrequented and mouth-watering mouth.

I can see you with them on your pillow later, counting them,
or moving them, this way and then this, thrilled

at their arrangements, smiling at a story, at their still sticky colours,
at the baby clicks they'll make even here,

out on their own, beyond their original home,
my butter mouth that pushed them into the world.

The Very Slow Train,

on the downhill stretch,
moves with the speed with which I grew
and with which I will, in my old age, shrink back
towards the warm and waiting ground—
myself a piston on its single push and pull,
among the billions more,
who grind this almost round world round.
And on the flat we slow to an adhered stamp's progress
across its envelope, or so it seems.
Whole yawning generations
come and go between two sleepers here.
And gazing out the window,
I watch a snail dart and flit beside the track.
The snail, which, before we reach our destination,
will have evolved, its descendents inhabiting shells
with living rooms papered in flock.
They'll rest their single feet on poufs.
They'll watch our train pull in
through windows mucus thin.
They'll see ourselves emerge as orbs of shining mind.
Please God, wait for me.

Emap in Australian Review

Emap is to review its Australian
consumer magazine business
and French exhibitions division.
The review was announced as part
of the company's commitment to
burning brown bees, pulled to the
(Oh, Gesundheit!) immolating honey.

They flare like little Fockers writing
HELP-LA-DI-DA and OH, SO SORRY
in the mad and some might say,
'fornicating' sky, their tiny souls
bailing out and coming down smiling.
Look closely at their faces.
They look exactly like me.

Carrier

She goes through water. She is made of bread,
beans, telephone conversations, milk, tea, music and shampoo.
Planes are on her decks. Like egrets on a hippopotamus;
like idiots, or children. Her flanks?
Well surely they are old and quite forgotten thoughts.

Her metal is thick. In the middle of each slab
it's as dark as it, one day, will be.
The weight would press you as thin as skin,
as thin as nothing. The anchor chains are of a monstrous toy.
The links hold each other

and where they touch is some awful pain.
Now look away and listen.
I think she is telling you something.
To be down here, in the silly, dark waves of the world's dull stomach;
the sticky surface, the clicking foam, the dirty smell of it.

Fact: the carrier's salted sides might be meat,
or my unhappiness, or my father, or something that for the moment,
slips my mind. They are going down underwater, going up above it.
Be sorry for it, please, because it's ours. I'm sure it is.
Yes, I am quite sure it is!

Carrier II

Come closer.
Come closer still, this time.
Right up against her hull.
Put your pink cheek on it,
close your tired eyes, little thing.

And be still, though you
may move your toes;
move your blind and infant moles
in the damp and dark at the shoe's end,
where upper's stitched to sole.

Yes, your rubbery and nourished tummy
will mime the carrier's pitch and roll.
Aye, her pitch and roll, Sir!
Ah, the cracking waves, Sir! The creaking waves,
on this forever undecided sea.

So rest your cheek upon her and know her to be true.
Unbending as she is. Driven as a cow,
by the stumbling men within,
whose aims are jolly and unknowing and unknown by her,
pushing on, above the plummeting deep of sea.

Carrier III (Peace)

He said to me,
we're not afraid of the warm nosed missile,
the charming bringer of itself, carrying itself as its gift,
a bottle which is a guest,
a moth grub rocket that makes quick holes
in the fabric of a boat, Sir.
Out here, displacing sea,
the unknowable foam, the sea a darkening
that draws and redraws itself correcting.
The waves toss and turn, bless them,
but we are on deck, among hard, stiff birds,
with our headphones playing us nothing,
holding our lollipops, we're barely sick with joy.

Carrier IV (In port)

Honestly, Sir, *he said,*
from in my painter's hanging cradle I have stared,
have barely rolled my wet, my quite aquatic eyes
(their looking coming out as fingers of anemones),
on small and varied parts of her enormous sides.
The metal seems, from here, as soft as painted canvas
(you can smell the oil still), the grey a mix of every colour
and every colour being, once upon a time, a thought.
I mean and wish to see so well
that I am able Sir, to find the colour's discrete parts;
to use my eyes as tongues to taste the single things
within the old (but still not rotten) stew.
And I ignore, and will, the foolish water underneath.
The light on it as little talk of friendly people in a bar.
The infant waves suck pointlessly.

As a Boy,

he saw God once, or his deed at least.
The sun coming down in a blessing—
the clouds part, the sun comes out,
the invisible angels sing an inaudible hymn,
that kind of thing.
And at other times he spoke to trees,
and them to him, or so he told me.
And in the meeting, last Tuesday,
in Conference Room 2,
he caught the pretty girl's eye,
composed a look meant to say,
How boring this is. And she smiled at him.
And his smile was slung from his ears,
making his face hot behind it.
And later in the toilets, he reprised his bored look,
and the smile and the eyes,
checking their effect in the mirror.
Age is coming down on him like a stone.

The King is in His Counting House

not counting out his money, but making some swanky
kind of love to his secretary,

her knickers clumped happily in his back pocket,
her behind positioned, not uncomfortably,

on the edge of the splendid, inlaid desk,
and collecting its superbly inconspicuous impression,

a barely discernible and effacingly transient
endorsement of its quality.

We may appraise later her bottom's embossment,
when she's had sufficient, and gets down from the table,

but for now, their shared and sumptuous sensations
are as turgid and as oiled as all the very eyes

that go about their business beyond the castle keep's
thick and stoned walls.

Yes, I'm afraid I've spent too long inside again,
when all I meant to show you was the Queen

eating sticky honey in the garden,
listening to the rummaging brook

and smiling at the small,
white joke of the sun's telling;

and the black bird watching the snub nose wriggle
in the middle of the maid's face.

Welcome to Disneyworld

It's hot in my suit
and I can't scratch
my itch
with my fat, white fingers.

And when I breathe in here
I can smell the smell
of last night's beer
and of Minnie.

She's standing over there.
Sometimes I think she looks at me
with her unblinking eyes
and her fixed smile.

The Sheets and Pillowcases

in this place, have a design printed on them
and he imagines the patterns might get up his nose while he sleeps,

that he'll feel them, rough on his cheek, or that they'll free themselves
from the fabric and slip beneath his eyelids,

to work their way around behind his eyes — open
behind their blinds of lids — and that they'll slice the optic nerve

to leave the marbles spinning, independent and random,
fleetingly pointing inwards, towards their severed cable, but unseeing,

as he is when he turns out the light and finds the sheets as smooth
on his skin as if they had been white.

Early this Morning,

and the flushed, embarrassed darkness
in its totally explicit nightie

is discovered hunkered in the bushes yet again
by the cheeky gleam of dawn.

And inside the condo, Marcie reads on the white
and paper page of 'Happy' Hooper's bedside copy

of *Positive Thought for the Day* that everything
in the whole world was made in the twinkling stars,

even Hooper's long and sleeping hands and this,
her pale and indigo waiting.

And Marcie's hopeless loving of me,
which I have made, is fading as she stands alone

in the teeming light of a rising, busy sun.

The Well-Dressed Street

wears Marcie—an accessory on its blue white noon.
Marcie wears the pressed uniform

of her comeliness over her ludicrous blood
full of its minute wheels.

She wears her smart body over her pocketed self,
her words under her scent,

her breath beneath her clothes, her heat
under the walloping sky. Her self is a long, translucent eel,

over which days pass, its tail at her birth, its brain here,
pushing the look of her along.

My Friend Marcie is on the Insensate Beach,

or by the dinking pool, or in the triumphant park.
She's sliding over pages of a magazine,

her scent is the scent of the sun: that stark and naked mistress,
who in her blinding coruscation, burns off her very own bikini,

who'll flash off underwear, a business suit and overcoat
quicker than she can summon them, already smouldering, to mind.

She's up there, bare as you like, her hair blazed to ash
and ash itself, in this blank heat, flared back to scratch,

before a damp and follicled root could jibber, blinking, into life,
before the quick, initial sting could even muster

to the judding pole of self. The alopecia sun, her porn star muff,
buff as these soft dreams I entertain of her,

my immolating, self-cremating angel,
who turns my coal-black words to molecules of slag,

who's salted tears cannot even jig as spit upon a frying pan.
She's squatting in her protest, her hollered rage at me,

her blasphemy, is in the shine on the magazine.
Its gloss is bouncing up all over Marcie like a rash.

Without Me, You're Nothing

Oh Marcie, Marcie,
trust me when I say I made you out of love.

Your body may be your own dream but you are mine.
I've watched you lie like a long branch of a tree,

I've watched you sleep
with the quiescent dreams of wood,

letting my very own denuded breath
move in and out of you, my Angel

and you ate it quietly as a child
(though now you take me in, as though it were I

that were the foundling).
Oh Marcie, I've watched you come half to yourself,

and forgive me if I watched you turn and,
Oh, say it! watched your body,

a scented buddy to yourself, your self's pork dolly,
dreaming its own fuckable dream.

There is So Much Green Idling in the Trees

The men are hunting deer,
their cars having pulled across particular gravel,
the gravel having welcomed the disturbance

and the long cars have the memory of homes reflected in them,
there is dust in the carpets picked up from sidewalks,
the seats smell of the men and their wives,

candy bar wrappers are as still as not to be there.
These happy cars, the engines click, they shrink to themselves.
And down in the forested ravine there will be stones

and a stream going round and over and under them
and light moving in its own way and the rattle of water.
The cars are unable to come down here

unless we were to lower them on cranes,
then their wheels would stretch for the rocky ground,
their chrome wing mirrors hurting at the love I'd shown for them.

Poor Derek,

whose lukewarm brain in my hot hand I hold.
What thought did slip across this soft wet stone,
did flare in an electric net of gold,
did cling, like a butcher's bag to this throne
of man? What filth, what porn was conjured here,
was collaged from cut pieces of the world,
from stolen ghosts of girls made to appear
in skin-flicks played on silver screens unfurled
like strips of cartilage within this nut
of thinking meat? What dirty dreams were dreamt
when Derek slept, his flicking eyelids shut,
the shell against the soft, sweet pillow leant
and in the shell, this brothel lying thus?
See it, as though he dreams again for us.

The Run

They're in the bath together.
Like tobogganists heading down and down a hill,
snow covering the land like a sleep.

He has his arms on the bath's enamel sides,
she, in her soft, transparent cap
is tweaking the cold control.

One day she may turn and find him gone.
Fallen off somewhere,
tumbling back towards the world.

I was Writing Recently on the Subject of Mice,

as it happens, those pale pink
and sudden morsels rolled in fur,

when at some unexpected moment,
I remembered you.

You came back to me, unbidden by association
(you weren't even wearing a coat).

And time as a fairground mirror
had twisted and delivered you to me not aged,

but as a freak-show creature
blinking at me hopefully.

And I saw that what once had seemed so faultless
had been itself

just an aberrant arrangement of matter,
a random knot in the fabric,

a place where the Universe came upon itself,
where it saw what it was made of and was afraid.

Look, From Where I'm Sitting at the Bar,

you can see the pleasure robots dance an ironic robot dance.
They look like queers to me, in the tight designer jeans

that are de rigeur among the pleasure machines.
But the real women seem to like them.

These divorcees who, in the robot's manufactured gaze,
slowly clock and anticlock their derrieres.

(Anticipating, as they no doubt do, the perfect screw,
the tranquilizer-laced ejaculate simulate.)

As for me, I am a model of a different kind.
With my greying hair, my silicon middle, my non-vibrating penis,

I am a commitment model and in the morning I'll be there.
When you come down the stairs, you'll find me standing in the kitchen,

gazing through the window at the darkness thinning in the dawn.
And you'll come up to me and touch my back

and ask if we drink coffee. And do you know, I've heard it said
that we're the ones who can be loved.

Though I believe that when you think you see my soul,
perhaps you only see my maker, for he is everywhere in here.

The Sausage Factory

is squeezing out bangers. Neat and hushed,
their sweet flesh pressed against skin windows,
they're coaxed out blinking

by tender midwives whose glove-squeezed fingers
have some of the familiarity of relatives.
With their unique arrangements of white fat freckles

they're glossy individuals, wee circus elephants,
gripping the tail of the one that goes before,
marching uncertainly away from death.

Be Careful,

while your eyes are turned away,
as some portion of attention
is taken by the sucking lustre of the bar—
the wood, the light, the brass, a homing dazzle;
then will he begin to talk and watch his words
work their crude and grunting magic on you.
His voice vibrating at your particular pitch,
will find out your resonance,
like the car which makes our bedroom window
rumble in its frame, he'll work on you,
your legs, the prongs of a tuning fork,
quivering your knickers down.

23

There is a silence like the sound of bells,
it's between things and it's in them, freeing
them of their names, which, like printed labels
slipped from submerged jam jars and now being
half things themselves, can no longer adhere
to the round world. Without their meanings, they
seem, in vain, to look for some purchase here,
in this smooth sea, where they'll forever stay,
while yellow underwater bells still ring.
And this is the place, just here, where the world's
lost and you're found with a hairdryer, a tin
of glue and a thin line, fishing for words.
But you are made of the sea. You're beheld
where its surface creases; where its waves fold.

The Bears are Skiing Through the Trees

Shush, shush, go the skis in the snow.
Oh, the concentrated glee across their furred faces!

Oh, oh, slicing that way! Oh, and slicing this!
Wanton smiles among the berries

and the honey in their stomachs.
Smiles like tiny, gravid bombs.

Chipmunks (which also should be hibernating)
watch from woody holes and wish

they had the wherewithal to clap their leather paws,
to holler piping hot and minute winter whoops!

Oh, how strange to find you here, touching your mouth
with icy fingers, the world's true cold on you.

This is for You

Concerned that you may be lost,
I put your name on a zeppelin.

It lay up there
like a stone

on the bottom of Hooper's
blue swimming pool.

Did you see that other me
holding my helium breath,

stuck, jutting against the sky,
wondering

if it's you I remember,
that heavenly animal burst,

my marvellously good idea
for a present?

Question 2

Do the wide-splayed flowers
in their rumpled beds
operate upon an insect portion of the brain—
a winged, dishevelled proto-bug trapped
in soft, grey amber?

And as a cabby's hippocampus,
crammed with avenue and mews, expands
in the manner of a muscle often used,
so have I grown a place behind my eyes,
where you reside?

Where you can watch the trees unfurling
and the grass going away, where you can sit
in the garden, on the roof of the shed,
with the pouring rain coming down
with its tranquilising certainty.

The Luxury Husbands are Working

The little wives,
small as rubber toys
stuck to the dashes of their SUVs,
their bottoms licked
to make them the better stick,
are driving round their district,

breathing special air.
Their hair is expensive.
They're smelling of fragrance.
Take them out.
Leave them for a while
and they'll smell of themselves.

George Said, Thinking is What the Dead Do,

they're stuffed with it, like bears are stuffed.
It's a rash that spreads, an empire on a map,
or tumbled milk on dirt, its whiteness abandoned,

becoming only wet. Where does that whiteness go?
Yes, *said Ulla, brightening, and touching George's knee,*
and dogs are cut from sheets of glass behind which

is a dog-like thing that barks!
And have you seen how clean it is behind the mirror's glass?
You could eat its anticlockwise dirt,

and when I was in the country, my spirit toppled out of me,
fell forwards from my pink and hopeful belly,
to be among the trees and the grass and the dew, my darling,

and to be home.
And Carl said with a grin that mice are words.
And we laughed. Oh, peals of it rising!

This is Me Speaking

Just to make that clear from the start.
So we know where we are. So we know who we are
and that I'm not just some invented clown,
some phoney alter ego. My name is Jean Pascin,

movie star, bon viveur, raconteur,
baiseur of the French sex-goddess in '54
in the hotel on the Côte d'Azur.
And people say to me,

Is it true, when you withdrew,
you found your biroute covered in a billion tiny stars
as though you'd dipped it in the night sky
and did she laugh to see them on you glinting

and were they on her clapping hands
and on the sheets and on your mouths
and did she cry like a child
because none of it is true, and did you?

From the Shore,

the gull and cormorant studded sea
is a dormant TV grey. Thick with salt,

it heaves with a slow and spastic restlessness,
mulling over crabs and stones;

though down in the dark and distant deep,
beneath the water's sulking press, it's all but still,

but for the sinking, plucked clean, secret bones of fish.
And gazing out, you find its weight pulls on you,

drags out your little thoughts, carries them
to a shore in Africa where bare and happy children

prod them in the brittle surf with sticks
and laugh at them.

The Sophisticated Odour of Love,

he continued, the bang-out-of-order odour of love,
deluxe, recherché, I have it all over me.

Yes, *she interjected*, it's even on the sudden,
blunt fish of my heart and here, on my pinkish lips.

Ah, *he uttered*, but surely it comes off both of us
like a shout, the prolific milk of hunger!

The horny, chunky air drops in and out of you.
You harvest it to fabricate the filmic smell of love.

When I watch you sleeping, deep inside your comeliness,
I know you're making more of it, for us to have later.

Microscopic Autumn

Way down beyond the world's
thin veneer of colour, black ridged fields of skin,
their hairs, cracked and bent trees,

flake to the canyoned floor
where grey boulders of dust
and juiceless prokaryotes lie in litter

disassembled to the edge of mathematics,
and our pink selves would choke and suffocate
on these revolving fists of oxygen.

This grey universe, a second moon,
rises underneath and presses us as flowers
within the pretty sliver where we live.

The Barman Turned

to me and I thought he said,
would you rather eat your own shit,
or a stranger's phlegm?

But apparently he'd said,
would you rather have a Carling or a Foster's?

And then I thought he said, *would you prefer*
to make careful love to a furious pig,
or to a girl's warm corpse,
her legs with the acquiescence of the innocent?

But apparently he'd said,
is that a pint or a half, chief?

And then I thought he said, *would you rather*
have your organs burst by a Daisy Cutter bomb,
or your head held down in the bathroom sink,
your tongue in vain stretching for the black plug's chain,
until you breathe the other world's thick breath?

But apparently he'd said,
Ready Salted or Cheese and Onion?

Baghdad Lockdown as Troops Hunt for Britons

Areas of Baghdad were under lockdown
yesterday as American and Iraqi troops
searched the city for the manner in which I loved you.
Forgive me then, that all that's left is the sheen
which I may find on a jittering leaf,
or the dead cat scream banging about
in the vixen's mouth, in the road outside.
Its heat is a dull bulb, the old town of the mind.
It's trotting where you once stood, when I cranked up
the bedroom window, its liquid pane still running.

Gunter is a Medium-Sized Bird

sitting on the front porch of the house in Dusseldorf.
He sings. He thinks the voluminous and billowing thought of men.
He wants to come inside, to rest upon the girl's behind,
as she, her body breathing, sidles up to sleep

(closing heavy doors, their bolts slipping home in her belly).
It's then that he will lift his head, lift his brittle beak to peck,
before he clatters up, scrambles through the full
and blooming air to the wardrobe top.

Her shout will overlap her waking and flicking over, she will laugh,
and he will jump claw to claw, calling, turning round and round,
scratching and skidding, making marks up there
where wanton time has built a dirty nest.

The hard, black feathers are on the tweeting bird.
Its body is hot like a battery. The tiny air, if you could hear it,
squeaks through its stiff nostrils. It does not mean you to take it
and its thin bones in your, forgive me, praying hands.

The One You See is Only a Replica

There are others,
identical in every important respect.

Each one mentions something reminiscent
of a flock of small birds scratching across a glass sky

and refers perhaps, to the trees
that rub themselves against a still, black wind,

and to the linings of gloves, and to a white car
that pulls its sound up a thin road.

Each alludes to the fur of difference like a mould
that grows on the edge of everything up close.

In the Space Between the Curtain

and the window
I found Our Lord
corrugated and still
slipping his mind under threads
smelling their filaments
inventing and retaining them
the sun, hot on his neck
the light (and all of this is of him)
eking into fabric
swimmingly ok and beautiful.
The dust, each mote
a piece of fruit in jelly, floats
as does our will in his.
Bless him!

Entropy

Oh I've considered being frozen, mulled over it,
sitting here, in the already nippy cold-store of my selfhood,

the hanging meat raging. Yes, I've looked at it, imagined
the damn and instant crack of freezing catch my eyes half-blinked,

their balls, pre-startled bon-bons, my soul
(in this particular dream, I have one) a frozen lake, further north

than man will ever tread, though ducks
will moon-walk on it, a look of twaddle playing on their bills.

But the problem is that even now, before I cross the potholed road
to post this in the chipped box, I move my pen, and spoil this page

with marks like the trails of delirious mice; and when I fold it,
I'll bend its minute fibres to my already sapping will.

Yes, even as I stick my stamp I'll nudge this wrinkled world,
this universe, towards its cold and this time quite eternal sleep.

Yes, Everything You Need is Here

A tree. Its branches creeping outward still,
their shape, the trails of their growing,
their growths' slow wakes.

Gravity. The downward going thought;
the crushing urge we have to hold each other;
the grunting destiny of stuff.

Rope. From a thousand little ropes entwined;
from the small, plain strength of homely strings,
the monstrous anger of the crowd.

We Think We See Richness, Said Dougal,

but in fact it's as thin as . . . as thin as . . .
Paper? ventured Florence, crossing and winding
her pretty legs. Her dark eyes

are ovals of infinite charm.
And Dougal felt, as he often did,
that he might topple into them and be wholly unfound
and that he'd find in there the other lost mutts
who fly and go in undulating packs,
forgetting why and longing
in a putty coloured piece of brain,
to be owned again,
and be more than what they have become—
nothing but her foaming happiness
rising in her as a swarm of barking pooch.

No, thinner than paper, said Dougal sadly.
I'm afraid there's nothing there at all,
we make it all up,
it forms in front of us as we go.

II

Dougal, though he never lived, is doubly dead
between the stop-frame camera's snide and bitter clicks.
Oh, some slow convection current might dink his fur,
but he is lifeless. And yet the Florentine dreams he cannot have
they happen here, when the dog is helpless, still and blind.
The dreams, they are that she is at the bar,
drinking more wine, smoking cigars with her black mouth,
her unknowing bottom on the barstool,
its imagined crease a marvellous little smile.
She winds her pretty legs, laughs her cotton laugh,
with the odorous, warm and trousered men about her.

III

He chews on his alone,
behind the flat tree.
He's been at it so long now,
it's as hard, and it's as dry
as a stone.

His unknown fears,
they accrue to another's—
to his rival's mythical bone,
until his seems vestigial
as an owned dog's brain.

And in this smooth garden,
the flowers haven't grown,
but come about.
They have happened
only in their own way.

IV

Forgive the flowers,
the hard flowers
who'll spin their magic waltz,
their contented, skimming dance.
I tell you, Dougal sees with dog and gimlet eye,
sees them flick against his unboned self.
Laugh, Sir! Madam, laugh, at the sliding dog!

But it observes more of the outside—
even through the eyes applied in paint.
And behind its made up face,
in its undone head, empty as a blown egg,
she sleeps, curled up in the darkness,
mistaken by the thing itself,
for its damned and doggy soul.

V

The dog has left no tracks at all!
He is slightly off-kilter on the sloping beach,
the waves coming in, the actual sun going down
and making his Japanese-white face, pink.
There are times when he feels her in him.
She's jammed him on like a lady's glove or a muff.
Forgive him. His dry tongue looks as though he longs
to lap, lap, lap. Yes, it's just as Brian said—
he worries away at her inside
like a dirty bad dog with a bone.

VI

It's quiet in the garden now and quite, quite still.
The magic night has cracked down,
and outsize dust from the other world
will fall tonight as a dry dew.
In his half and dogged sleep, Dougal sees her crunchy,
her crunching eyes wetted and widening
until they gape and screech at him, and bang and bark
and stamp and tear and break.
And he is holding Florence flailing on a cracking leash,
as though her longing were bestial
and he a pink and hopeless man.

VII

No, you can't die Dougal, not even when all the lights have set
and the world beyond turns on its axle as silent as a ghost,

quiet as this lack of what might be called love. Forgive us,
that the world is as flat as a map of it, that beyond it

is nothing you can know, my sorry dog who has been,
but has not lived in here, all these umbilical years. Even now,

I see the unmanned shock, the un-dogged shock, in your made-up face
at being no more than the dry and petty stuff of which you're made,

and the transmission of the image of it, that once upon a time,
had seemed at least to have the smell of blood about it.

VIII

My dear Sir, or should I say Monsieur,
said Dougal in an email,

can I just say what a pleasure it's been to work with you,
it's been enormous fun, 'an absolute hoot'

as Brian might put it. I particularly liked the way
you portrayed us in the style of a '50s Western,

the big skirts, the tinkly clank of spur
on wooden floor, the sun going down like a pink lolly

and, let's face it, the wonderfully sexy weight of the guns.
I absolutely loved the campfire scene,

the way the light danced on me, as though those shadows
expressed something of the crazed, the rabid sorrow

behind my face. My face that, just as you taught me,
does almost nothing—nothing more than let itself be taken.

ix (Time for Bed)

I agree, that though he knew that it could never be,
he longed to have her, with his imaginary penis
more that of a man than a dog
and made from a discarded loo roll tube
whose absorbency would necessitate the use of a condom
which Florence would apply as though she prepared a delicacy
or dressed a baby, her oval eyes dilating.
Please don't get him wrong,
Dougal meant, in part at least, to stroke or jolt her soul with it,
to free her sadness which he would hold for her
and show her like a bunch of magic flowers.

He's Face Down in the Lake

arms out as though he's going *Come here*
and let me hug you, or he's asking *Why?*

his arms describing the size of the question,
or he's been crucified and nailed to the sky,

or he's folding an invisible sheet,
or surrendering perhaps, or closing a window,

or conducting an orchestra, holding some piece of quiet
between his fingers, or letting it go,

or he's bowing before an idol,
going *I am not worthy Master.*

Or he's looking for something
down here among the water weeds,

a lost ring his wife gave him,
he's thinking *She'll kill me.*

Listen,

he spoke her then and speaks her now,
her name, a bone immersed

inside the cotton of his exhalation,
so little meat on it, but some. Some,

in the fleeting weight of vowel in his throat,
he eats on that for sure,

before he lets its smoke and ash out
upon his breath.

And he might sometime speak her name
inside his shut mouth. Without its consonant

it's crippled to a sound of pleasured grunt
that mocks him with the absence of her touch.

In the Park

where poofters, as we knew them, lingered
as sorry boners in the dusk, I found the Lord.
I knew him by his invisibility and his smile.
He was beneath the tree
and may have been its soul.
Certainly something sappy smiled and bloomed
and hung and saw me, no more than a boy.
And going home,
I saw the braking lights of cigarettes
as they sucked on them
in the bitter shadow of his glory.

It's in Black and White

and I've cast Gary Cooper.
His character's name is George.
George looks up at the man at the bar.
And says a line about how he's a nobody.

He says (forgive me if I don't do the accent),
he says: *I'm a nobody.*
I get him to say it again.
I'm a nobody he says.

And he looks back down at his hands
and his whisky the colour of lead.
That's what a star can give you,
you can feel the world's little jolts.

Juice

I saw my helpless, raw, unguilty blood
sweep the barrel of its sweet-tempered smack
(the poppies' woody recompense m'lud).
I flushed it of each last remnant of sap
and slowed to the pace of the sleeping trees
who've never learned our queer, our swindling trick
of crawling on the earth as an ill breeze.
Since then I find the words I use toxic.
The things I said before were true to touch
but now I find my mouth and my dulled eyes
a stage for made-up fools, buffoons, and such
whose lip-stuck smiles are dry as husks of flies.
Still less alive than my own running juice,
my extraction, my descent—my excuse.

I Called the Plumber to Say, the Lavatory
Does Flush,

but it hasn't got its heart in it, it never quite
engages, or reaches culmination,

but spends its reservoir wastefully
on its voiding shrug of an emission.

It's a sad sack splutter of a sneeze; or it's a yawn,
the beguiling chasm of which you're just plunging into,

when you're snagged in the branches of a raggedy bush;
or an orgasm has rung the front door bell

and when you answered it, expecting that wonderful
fancy dress costume, he's gone,

disappearing down the street and round the corner,
his outfit looking ridiculous at this distance;

or it's a hopelessly damp, a miserably oh, whatever.

In the Garden, Birds in Feather Masks

hop or walk around the gravel paths
and the trees come out of the ground.
It's about 3:30 on Thursday, the sky is blue
and the brown dog is at the back door all over again.
Isn't he strange. He is mouse small,
with eyes as small as holes made by tiny nails.
He holds his head to one side and looks at you

and you wonder if he wants the glass of water
you're holding in your white hand, my darling.
The old wind is in the trees, tickling them,
tripping over the lawn you mowed
the Sunday before the Sunday before last,
getting inside your blouse like a clumsy thief,
flicking the little dog's fur.

The Dining Table

is in the field —
an itch, a sudden curtailed

scent, sex with a stranger,
a moment's

pandemonium, she said.
But when he turned to her

to say, *Pardon?*
he found she wasn't there.

It had been a kind of
dream, a soft world coming in,

something badly
translated,

a bruise in the apple,
a parrot on snow.

Their Lobes, Like Earrings, Hang

Ears look passive but also greedy.
They take without giving, they hear but never speak,
listen and never whistle. They're gristle,
nearly genital in the goofiness of their design
and in the way they amplify.
They're seeing even when you're sleeping.
They sit outside the cave as guards,
waiting for a prehistoric dawn to wake you
with the yellow-pink of eyelid light.
They pass the time in dumb and rudimentary games
or by drawing simple scribbles in the sand
by the light of a slightly smoother moon.
Then suddenly they drop their sticks, they run inside,
grab you by the shoulders, and you wake
and stare at them imploringly, earless as you are.

Would You Excuse Me Madam,

would you forgive me? I have something peculiar
that belongs to the Major.

I thought I might describe it for you.
Make it, if not hallucinatory, for that is what it is,

then at the very least, warmer than this tepid page of paper,
this mere wrapper for the thing itself.

For it is beneath this sheet and my rubbing pen
moves over it

as though it were a brass that seems to stir
beneath the tickling jibbers of my nib,

or as if it were a coin of some perverse denomination,
exchangeable only for bone or rumour,

the ruler's head smiling under my fastidious,
repetitive scribble.

And now we find its twitch beneath the sheet,
will you touch or hold it even,

as its owner, the moustachioed Major, falls away
and loses focus, his cap, no more than a smudge?

I Suppose You Could

take the paper down these quiet stairs, go out
onto the stiff, black road, take a taxi to the station
where the tracks end in their frustrated flourishes of iron.

You could go to the countryside and there,
beneath some ravenous sky, drag it across the fields.
You could take the sheet of paper

and bending down, pull it through the grass.
There's certainly nothing on it as un-damned
as the scratch of a stick, a stain of sap,

a streak of dew, an insect, smaller and harder
than the dot of an i, or the soft crease you put in it
with your own hand as you held it to the good ground.

Look, My Love,

the duck they are a-laying again! The billed, be-feathered duck,
they lay the plenished eggs that sleep untroubled sleep.
You may touch their gritty shells, you may clutch
the laden weight of them. You may boil and peel a pair—
and I might suggest you keep 'em peeled, for their whites
are the blue-white white of the whites of eyes,
and raw, that albumen's the vitreous, the jelly humour
where the pictured world is yoked to us.
Oh, sit on these my eyes, my darling! Hatch what I will see!

His Hand is in My Head

His fingers roll the dark sides of my moon eyes,
or they make my mouth move as my mouth moves now.
Sometimes he sticks out his thumb
pressed into my tongue and makes me kiss you,

my eyes as surprised as candy beneath their drawn down lids.
On occasion I have felt his bumping knuckles nudge
my quite stiff brain in its bowl, tipping it a little,
making it pull against my stretching spine, making my toes curl.

There's a Small, Blurry Dog Jumping Up and Down and Barking

Above him is a little swarm of green bluebottles.
The green's so bright and beautiful it skips your eyes

and comes to rest a long way in,
somewhere near the region where you laugh.

The devil's eyes might be this colour, as shiny as this.
You could see yourself in them, stretched in their curvature,

in this squeaky green they make from excrement and rot.
You'd find yourself thinking

they'd look lovely shrunk, as beads, or not shrunk, as gobstoppers.
You'd imagine sucking one at work, as a socket sucks an eye,

pulling back your lid-like lips to make your colleagues screech,
as though the very colour punched out a bob of air.

You'd make your green eye blink as though surprised.
You'd dribble as though you cried.

It's Hard Work, Pulling the Ghost Out of a Man

It clings like a child will cling to its favourite toy.
It stamps and pleads and rages

and cries and bites and, in desperation, even laughs.
It grips the inside of the man's face

and as you prise one hand of fingers free,
it strengthens its hold with the other.

And as you yank and yank it by the ankles,
it'll clutch at collar bone and then each rib in turn

as it comes gradually down the ladder,
more despairing with each rung,

its swearing turning quieter as it begins to tire
and turns its white coloured stare on your own ghost,

turned away inside you,
apparently engaged in some private matter.

The Brand New Dark is Getting In,

the speed boats are of the sweetest and wonderful knives,
the clouds and the cranes on the docks—

strips of black leather inlaid in the metal green sky,
the whole thing just sitting back there.

She moves her allure across the engine's holler and
touches the man's liquorice carbine.

She speaks to him and the wind pulls back her hair
and her whole baby skin just tugged up by it.

The boats are holding themselves,
they cry like Jesus on a brittle world;

the guns are so inky and homeless and infant;
everything is loving everything else

and the wakes are softly bleating white now,
and letting it go, stone hard and gone.

Sometimes I remember who I am.

Be Quiet,

be still.
Let your hands rest on your paddles,
let your skin-canoes slow
and listen to the sound of the swamp.
The water thinking about itself,
the trees stood in it.
And know how the manatees
are down there underneath,
arranging and rearranging themselves
into what we might call stories.